# FINDING GOD IN
# ANIME

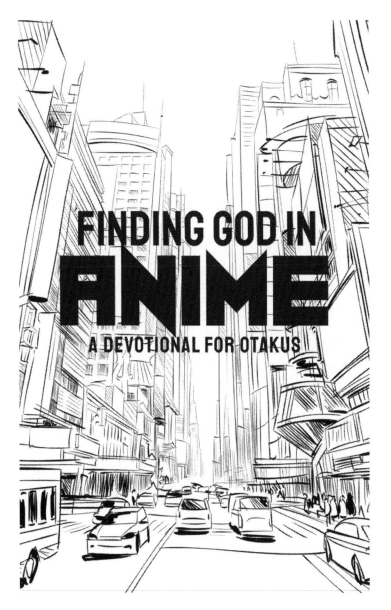

# FINDING GOD IN
# ANIME
## A DEVOTIONAL FOR OTAKUS

Cover design by Joanna Alonzo          Internal artwork by Beano-Chan
Edited by Angela R. Watts              Formatted by Selina R. Gonzalez

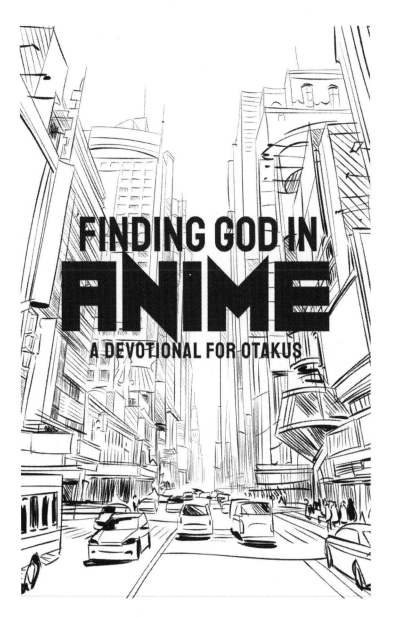

# FINDING GOD IN
# ANIME
## A DEVOTIONAL FOR OTAKUS

Cover design by Joanna Alonzo      Internal artwork by Beano-Chan
Edited by Angela R. Watts           Formatted by Selina R. Gonzalez

*To all the otaku who are on fire for Jesus,*
*may you continue to burn bright.*

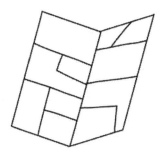

# TABLE OF CONTENTS

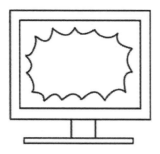

# INTRODUCTION

こんにちは (Hello)! A warm welcome to you, fellow otaku, as you have picked up this devotional! In this book, we otaku band together in our mutual love for all things anime and a desire to grow in our relationship with God.

In this devotional, you will find God in the animes you love—whether it be shoujo or shounen. Each devotional is penned with a different theme in mind. You may discover how to conquer fear in *Attack on Titan* or practice purity in *Sailor Moon*. Whatever your favorite show may be, and whatever area in your walk with the Lord you need encouragement in, it is our hope that these bite-size devotionals will be the toast in your mouth after running late to school: nourishing despite the high speed and stress of life!

# FAMILY LIKE *FAIRY TAIL*

## BY E.N. CHAFFIN

If there was one anime that I would vote for in the category of "has the best family," it would be *Fairy Tail* hands down. Why? A viewer would have to look no farther than the main guild for which the show is named after. Most of the members of *Fairy Tail* don't have families of their own and have, in one way or another, come to join the guild. They don't join just to gain power or prestige, like with other guilds in the show. They join to be a part of a family. This family of theirs is rowdy and nothing like the ideal perfect family some people have in their minds. However, they protect each other, they make sure every member is taken care of, and they never forget those who have gone astray or who have passed away. They are their own support system.

God tells us to "Be devoted to one another in love. Honor one another above yourselves. Never lacking in zeal, but keep your spiritual fervor, serving the Lord. Be joyful in hope, patient in affliction, and faithful in prayer. Share with the Lord's people who are in need. Practice hospitality," (Romans 12:10-13, NIV). We are also told to "Keep on loving one another as brothers and sisters. Do not forget to show hospitality to strangers, for by so doing some people have shown hospitality to angels without knowing it. Continue to remember those in prison as if you were together with them in prison, and those who are mistreated as if you yourselves were suffering," (Hebrew 13:1-3, NIV). Sound familiar, doesn't it?

Throughout the series, the *Fairy Tail* guild members exhibit all of these attributes. Even when former enemies like Gajeel and Juvia become a part of the guild, they are accepted. Yes, there are times when members get into fights with one another, but they always get past it and grow stronger in the process. Christians, the children of God, need to do the same with one another.

So take it from *Fairy Tail* and treat your family as God wants you to treat them—with love, respect, and acceptance.

# RELIANCE

## BY MEGAN DILL

Two are better than one, because they have a good reward for their toil. For if they fall, one will lift up his fellow. But woe to him who is alone when he falls and has not another to lift him up! Again, if two lie together, they keep warm, but how can one keep warm alone? And though a man might prevail against one who is alone, two will withstand him—a threefold cord is not quickly broken.

— Ecclesiastes 4:9-12 (ESV)

Have you ever heard the expression "two heads are better than one"? The concept of people working together to accomplish something has been around for a while; it's even mentioned in the Bible! When people work alone, it's easy for them to get overwhelmed or even fail. Not to mention, there are just some things in life that you're not meant to do alone!

A relay race is a great example of something you can't do alone. The race is divided into sections or laps and a team of runners takes turns running their designated part. In *Run with the Wind*, Haiji wants to participate in a famous marathon relay race. However, he needs a team of ten in order to enter the race. Without nine other people, he won't even get a chance to participate! Realizing that he can't run it alone, he recruits other members to his team. Each runner has their strengths and weaknesses, so the team members each run the section most suited to their skills. By dividing the race up between the runners, the members are able to do what they never would have been able to do alone!

Similarly, humans are not designed to go through life alone! Obstacles and challenges will come and go, and we're not meant to face them on our own. We have a powerful and mighty God on our side who is *always* there for us! In addition, we can rely on other believers! The body of Christ is full of prayer warriors who can provide us with comfort and strength. They can give godly advice, offer their support, and work with us through challenges!

God has also given us different gifts. Like the runners who each have their different strengths and weaknesses, we can overcome our weaknesses if we work together! We can each handle the responsibilities and challenges that are best suited to our skills. A team with a diverse skill set can accomplish more than one person ever could!

Haiji was able to realize that he would need assistance if he ever wanted to fulfill his dream. We should also acknowledge that we weren't created to do everything on our own—we have God Himself and an entire spiritual community to rely on and work together with!

# FINDING FAITH IN *THE PROMISED NEVERLAND*

## BY MORIAH JANE

Rather than using clever and persuasive speeches, I relied only on the power of the Holy Spirit. I did this so you would trust not in human wisdom but in the power of God.

— 1 Corinthians 2:4b-5 (NLT)

Emma is far from eloquent. Anyone who has watched the anime or read the manga for *The Promised Neverland* knows this. Unlike her two best friends Ray and Norman, she doesn't detail her plans in complex mathematical equations or brain-bending yet witty strategies. Even though she lacks these capabilities, she has one capability that trumps all the others: faith.

Devastations meet Emma's trio time and time again, but she never loses faith. When she and Norman discover the terrible secret of the Gracefield orphanage, she keeps the faith that they can change their deadly fate. When Norman and Ray try to convince Emma that escaping with all the orphans of Gracefield is highly improbable, Emma insists that there must be a way to ensure each orphan's escape, keeping the faith deep within her heart that they will all find freedom together. Yes, again and again Emma is met with soul-crushing odds and situations that would cause anyone to lose faith, yet she never does.

In this way, Emma is demonstrating the example set in 1 Corinthians 2:4-5. She relies on the personal faith she has mustered that somehow, someway, their horrifying reality will be resolved. She does not trust in human wisdom which often tells her that escaping her deadly destiny is impossible, that all her loved ones will slowly die one after the other, or that the situations she becomes ensnared in while against supernatural odds will be the end for her. No, she keeps fighting. And no matter what her enemies do to her, no matter what logic or science dictates, Emma presses forward with her eyes on the prize.

While reading *The Promised Neverland* and witnessing Emma's strong faith, I couldn't help but be reminded of our faith in Christ. Sometimes having faith is hard. We don't understand why trials have befallen us or how we'll ever make it through a difficult time. But Colossians 3:2 tells us to keep our minds on the things from above. In difficult times, we must keep our eyes on Jesus and on the good times in heaven still to come—our prize.

Emma shows great faith in every trial just as we ought to as Christians. If our friends tell us the odds are insurmountable, keep the faith. If the enemy seems too large and fierce, keep the faith. When we're tempted to focus on the things of earth, look up and keep the faith.

Always keep the faith.

# THE TITAN WITHIN

## BY ANGELA R. WATTS

We all have titans within ourselves. "Titan" roughly means: something large in size or power, standing out for greatness or success. Maybe we struggle with addiction, or pride, or fear, or anything that holds us back from Jesus. How do we fight the darkness?

My brother and I are watching *Attack on Titan* season 1 while waiting for season 4 to release weekly (torture!). I'm struck by the consistent theme of courage and hope interwoven through this violent, seemingly hopeless series.

Captain Levi—a central character—has always driven me forward. While I struggled with life during my pre-teen and teen-hood years, I wanted to have a steadfast strength... like Levi. I wanted to be unyielding, protective, and there for those who needed me. I didn't want to care how others viewed me or allow fear to guide me.

*"Endure it. Don't let go."*
— Armin Arlert

*Attack on Titan* is dark and if you're not looking for hope, you probably won't see it. Isn't that how normal life is? The demons in your mind will take reign and smother your hold on Jesus. If you're not fighting for hope and courage, it will not show itself.

When my mother was chronically ill and we thought we'd lose her, I told myself, "The fight isn't over. Keep fighting." When I've faced rejection and lost friends, I told myself, "Keep fighting, keep moving on." The ability to fight, no matter physical or spiritual, is something that drives me and comes naturally. But I've started struggling with the fear, is my fighting all in vain?

*Attack on Titan* makes me ask all sorts of questions: What would I do in this situation? Would I be strong enough to handle that? More often than not, my answer is, "No. I couldn't." That's the key—alone, we are hopeless. We are weak. The demons within us, the voices pulling us down, the titans before us... they are all too much for us to handle. Even Levi had his breaking points and I related strongly to that!

But because of Jesus, we are never alone. God can use anything for His good. We do not have to fear or succumb to the titans within or surrounding us. Yes, life is hard, and it will break us down and tear us apart. That's okay. All that matters is we get up and fight again. As humans, we all have our struggles, ongoing or short-lived, big or small. Trials are a part of life. But Attack on *Titan* reveals that no matter the size or type of trial, we do not give in. We do not back down.

Behold, we count them happy which endure.
Ye have heard of the patience of Job, and have seen
the end of the Lord; that the Lord is very pitiful,
and of tender mercy.
—James 5:11 (KJV)

If we surrender our weakness to the Lord and then fight what battles He gives us to fight... We can rest in Him, we can fight for His Kingdom, and we can rejoice in His love. Why? Because the ultimate battle is won! This doesn't mean we won't have battles or wars to fight. This doesn't mean He doesn't need us to fulfill our purpose here on earth. But it does mean we can hold onto hope, and courage, and faith, knowing that He is always with us. Our strength comes from God!

So, fight. Don't allow fear or your struggles to define you or keep you down. Seek God's strength, love, and guidance, and move forward. God has a purpose for you. He will heal your broken pieces. Fight the good fight and never give up! As Mikasa says, "You don't stand a single chance to win, unless you fight."

# NAUSICAÄ AND THE OHMU

## BY JESSICA BERTRAND

Rage turns the corners of our vision gray and causes us to see red. That kind of anger begs to be appeased by force. It won't leave until the agitator is left bleeding or dead. The Ohmu felt this sort of fury often. As protectors of the Toxic Jungle, the Ohmu's swift vengeance came to any who hurt or seemed to abuse an insect. Their normal blue eyes spark red and they go on a rampage. If the infraction is severe enough, the whole herd becomes involved and the hoard won't stop until the city is razed to the ground or they starve to death.

We must take care in our own lives when dealing with passionate and explosive emotion. James 1:19-20 (RSB) says, "This you know, my beloved brethren, but everyone must be quick to hear, slow to speak and slow to anger; for the anger of man does not achieve the righteousness of God." Anger is an emotion, and it has its place. It is reasonable to be upset without it becoming a sin, however, caution must be used so our relationship with God isn't affected.

Anger flashes, like a firecracker, and when it's gone destruction is left in its wake. Nausicaä time and again had to work with the Ohmu to keep them from outrage. The trouble with this volatile reaction, is it can rub off on those who try and help. Proverbs 22:24-25 (RSB) states, "Do not associate with a man given to anger; or go with a hot-tempered man, or you will learn his ways and find a snare for yourself." Nausicaä found out what flash rage did, and it took Lord Yupa to help her out of it. The result devastated her and changed her whole outlook on life. What will it take for us to see the sin in our own lives?

There is forgiveness when we make mistakes as we are all in different stages of maturity. God doesn't expect us to be righteous on our own. Jesus came to die for all our sins, including the everyday ones we don't see as problematic. As we grow in our understanding in Christ, it becomes easier for our red eyes to change back to blue like the Ohmu. Let's take it to the Lord.

*Come now Jesus and be our guest. If it weren't for you, I wouldn't be here. Thank you for your forgiveness when I make mistakes. Help me to acknowledge when anger is nearby and hold tightly to You until it passes. In Jesus' name I pray, amen.*

# DEKU'S TRUE QUIRK

## BY C.O. BONHAM

*My Hero Academia* is an anime where 80% of the population has a superpower, called a quirk. The Protagonist, Izuku Midoriya, starts out without a quirk. Luckily, All Might, the world's greatest hero, can pass on his quirk, One-for-All.

Izuku takes on All Might's power, but he didn't need it. He already had a God given quirk, that he uses to strengthen not himself but others.

Izuku adopts the name Deku (one who can't do anything) as his hero name, a nickname given to him in childhood because of his quirkless nature. Even before receiving the One-for-All quirk, Izuku shows through his actions that he *can* do anything. Izuku watches heroes and learns about their powers, he can analyze their strengths and weaknesses and can assesses how best to use them. How best to strengthen them.

Even when One-for-All would have enabled him to smash his way out of a fight. Izuku stops, he assesses, and he helps. He knows exactly what is wrong with each person he meets. He sees what is weighing on their hearts and he teaches them how to be the best versions of themselves.

The best example of this is in the season two episode "Shoto Todoroki: Origin." In this episode, Izuku is taking part in a sports competition, and he has to face off against his classmate Todoroki.

Todoroki has two quirks, fire and ice. But he will only use his ice power inherited from his mother. He refuses to compete with his father's fire powers out of protest for how his father abused his mother.

So Deku had the advantage, right? His opponent has walked out onto the field with a voluntary handicap. But Izuku doesn't wipe the floor with this guy. He talks to the guy while they fight. He reminds Todoroki that it isn't his father's ability, it's his. The only one punished by Todoroki holding onto his anger is himself.

In the end, not only does Izuku loose, because Todoroki has embraced his full power, but Todoroki ends up reconciling with both his parents.

Deku's quirk is more like Jesus than All Might's.

Jesus doesn't come around offering to give us exceptional power and fame. He talks to us, analyzes us, and teaches us how to be our best selves. He then empowers us to do the same for others.

Each superhero gives their quirk a catchy and descriptive name, like One-for-All. If I were to name Deku's quirk, I would call it: Build up others.

Is this your quirk, too?

**Therefore encourage one another and build each other up, just as in fact you are doing.**
**— 1 Thessalonians 5:11 (NIV)**

# PURITY

BY AMY LYNN MCCONAHY

Don't let anyone look down on you because you are
young, but set an example for the believers in speech,
in conduct, in love, in faith and in purity.
— 1 Timothy 4:12 (NIV)

Purity is a strong theme in the anime *Sailor Moon*. This
anime follows a fourteen-year-old girl named Serena
Tsukino, who becomes Sailor Moon the leader of the
Sailor Scouts. Serena has many character flaws including
laziness, irresponsibility, and whining, just to name a
few. Though these flaws are humorous, these are not

traits that most would want to see in their leader. In the show Serena redeems these flaws by being "pure of heart". Time and again, when the Sailor Scouts found themselves in a battle with great evil, her purity of heart would save the day. Believe it or not, the use of purity to conquer evil is a theme in the Bible as well. Jesus' purity, lack of sin, combined with His willingness to sacrifice Himself in our place gave Him the power to defeat the devil. Now, it is true that Serena was not truly pure, without sin, and neither are we. We all have flaws, but as Christians we should strive to live as purely as we possibly can by reflecting the purity of Jesus. Psalm 119:9 (NIV) says, "How can a young person stay on the path of purity? By living according to your (God's) word." Jesus stayed pure by following the laws sent down from God. These commandments can be boiled down to this simple truth found in Matthew 22:37-40 (NIV), "Jesus replied: "'Love the Lord your God with all your heart and with all your soul and with all your mind.' This is the first and greatest commandment. And the second is like it: 'Love your neighbor as yourself.' All the Law and the Prophets hang on these two commandments."

How can you show purity in your own life? Love God and Love your neighbors. This makes purity both the most difficult to achieve as well as the most simple to understand. I pray that you strive, undaunted, toward achieving purity in your life today.

# WE DON'T NEED THE MEMORIES

### BY LAURA A. GRACE

Have you dwelled on a stupid decision longer than you wanted to? One not from yesterday or even the day before that. No, it's the one memory from years ago that comes back in all its haunting glory.

It sticks around after its "appearance" like a piece of dirty gum on the bottom of your shoe. And when we try to peel it off, it refuses to unstick and come off. The memory instead continues to cling to our minds; once again making us relive all the pain of that poor decision, despite if the person or people have forgiven us or even if we've forgiven ourselves. In the wake of experiencing those emotions all over again, it can lead to questioning and doubting if we *really* deserved forgiveness, grace, or mercy in that situation the first time (or even second and third times).

When the fourth season of *Haikyu!!* aired, I remember being very intrigued that Inarizaki's team banner read, "We Don't Need the Memories." What an interesting concept for a championship team! I recall thinking that memories aren't necessarily a bad thing to relive—that is until I start dwelling on a bad memory. No one really wants to relive those kinds of memories over and over, and even the Bible encourages us not to dwell on the past. "Forget the former things; do not dwell on the past. See I am doing a new thing!" (Isaiah 43:18-19a, NIV).

As hard as it can be to let those memories go when they awaken feelings of personal loathing and disappointment, we can cling to the truth that when we gave our hearts to Jesus, He indeed did something new in us! "The old has gone, and the new is here" (2 Corinthians 5:17, NIV), and that includes freedom from memories that come to the surface and try to make us doubt and question our worth, our identity in Christ. The memories of yesterday or a year ago do not define who we are. We can know this with certainty because Lamentations 3:22-23 tells us, "Because of the Lord's great love we are not consumed, for his compassions never fail. They are new every morning; great is your faithfulness" (NIV).

I dare you to jump as high as you can and spike the ball as hard as you can, while cherishing the truth that you are a son or daughter of God and that no bad memory could ever rob you of this timeless truth.

May you race forward with absolute boldness and faith that is free from anything that should try to weigh you down, bad memories and all.

# CREATOR VS CREATED

## BY KANDI J WYATT

### For your personal reading: Genesis 3:1-24

A tale as old as time—and no, it's not Beauty and the Beast, that's a different genre. This tale is one of the Creator being challenged by one of His created. In *Re:Creators* the theme of creator vs created rings loud and true. From the very first episode to the end, the whole premise is that anime, video game, and manga characters should rise up against their creators because the creator doesn't know what's right for them.

Does that sound familiar? All the way back in the Garden of Eden, the created did the same thing. Satan asks Eve if God really said what he said. When she responds with a twisted truth, he tells her it's not true, "For God knows that when you eat of it your eyes will be opened, and you will be like God, knowing good and evil," (Gen 3:5 ESV).

See how that's so close to what Altair tells Selesia, Meteora, Mamika, and all the other characters that she brings into the real world? The Military Uniform Princess meets each created being as they come into our world and tries to sway them, telling them their creators are morons who know nothing about what life is really like.

And yet, that is exactly what Satan does today. There's not a character in a red suit with a pitchfork, or an angel in a military uniform that comes to us and calls us to question our trust in our Creator, but those little quiet moments of doubt, or the full-on assault from the media whispers, "Does God *really* know what's best for you?" It's part of that "pride of life" John mentions in 1 John 2:16.

In the end, the created has nothing to say to the creator. It's like the pot asking the potter, "Why did you make me this way?" (See Romans 9:19-24 and Isaiah

36

29:15-16) It's foolishness to think we can stare at God and shake our fist saying He doesn't know. Instead, He could look at us and call us *baka*.

> *"The Military Uniform Kid, she said that this is a*
> *world of the gods. A world where anything can be*
> *created with words. And that if I find the creator of my*
> *world, remaking my world would be a piece of cake."*
> —Yūya Mirokuji, *Re:Creators*

# "PIKACHU, I CHOOSE YOU!"

## BY LAURA A. GRACE

Many of us have probably heard those iconic words spoken by Ash as well as seen the multiple Pokémon plushies, trading cards, and clothing in stores and online. Like many children, when Pokémon took the world by storm, you might have even grown up collecting the cards and aspired to be a Pokémon trainer with your own Pokémon battles in your backyard.

Having been one of those children growing up, it was little surprise when *my children* wanted to wear Pokémon gear and have Pokémon themed birthday parties. After a recent birthday with said theme, I had received a comment from someone online stating that I should not be writing manga due to not being Japanese. The commenter scoffed, saying they would never read a manga made by a non-Japanese creator. They said I should have listened to the articles I had read that claim manga creators must be Japanese.

It was hard not to become angry and stop the trail of thoughts voicing how wrong they were to say such a thing that followed. I thought of all the aspiring manga creators such as myself who longed to see our stories in manga format but might stop pursuing that dream because someone said we could not due to our ethnicity. However, as upset as I was concerning this person's words, I strongly felt the Holy Spirit putting on my heart that I could choose to speak in love to this person, that I could choose to be joyful—or I could let resentment and disgust for their words burn in me.

This eventually led me to thinking about Ash and how he too can relate. On several occasions, Ash has been told that he will never become a great Pokémon trainer. He's either too young, too inexperienced, or lacks enough strong Pokémon to win. This was especially true when Ash chose his very first Pokémon, but in each of those moments, Ash made a choice. He could choose to dwell on these people's words and give up on his dream of being an aspiring Pokémon trainer, or he could have faith that even if he was too young, too inexperienced, and didn't have the "strongest" Pokémon, that he could still give it his all and *be* a Pokémon trainer.

And ultimately, he did.

From the first time Ash made the choice to pick up the Poké Ball that held Pikachu, he continuously ignores the doubts and the mockery of others who would say he or his Pokémon will never be good enough.

We can make a similar kind of choice in the situations we face day-to-day. That day I received that comment, I could have responded in fierce anger to this person who said I could not pursue this God-given dream of encouraging readers through Christian manga. I could have wallowed in doubt that maybe, just maybe, the voices like theirs were right and give up. But Paul encourages us in 1 Timothy 6:12a with this: "Fight the good fight of the faith," (NIV).

We may not be deciding which Pokémon to send out in battle next, but we *are* having to make the active and serious decision in deciding if we will "suit up" by putting on the armor of God. We are not simply fighting against other people's words. No, Paul tells us it goes much deeper than that in Ephesians 6:12 (NIV) and that the only way we can combat the power of those words that would try to drown out our callings is by following the verse that follows.

**Therefore put on the full armor of God, so that when the day of evil comes, you may be able to stand your ground, and after you have done everything, to stand.**

May you stand strong fellow warrior and trainer! May you take heart in knowing that God has chosen *you* and has not rejected you (Isaiah 41:9b, NIV), so may we, in return, *choose* to stand firm in our faith, in our God, and carefully place on our armor each day so we may be ready to face tomorrow, regardless of the trial or hardship.

# NOT BY MY MIGHT

## BY HANNAH CARTER

I am the type of person who likes to do everything themselves. I like to have control, and I like to have everything *just so*. If there's a problem, *I* need to fix it. And I need to do it—because I am self-reliant and I can believe in my own strength.

But there's one thing I can't seem to do by my own strength.

*I can't save or fix myself.*

No matter how hard I try, I feel like Paul in Romans 7, where he says that the things he wants to do, he can't, and the things he doesn't want to do, he does.

Yeah. I hear you, Paul.

But you see, in this "relying on myself" attitude, I miss one key feature: *I literally can't do it by myself.*

This reminds me of Deku from *My Hero Academia* in the first few episodes. Deku had the desire to be the best version of himself he can be (aka, a superhero), but had no way to achieve it. All by himself, Deku, like me, is pretty pathetic. He's got the willpower to change but no way to achieve that change.

Enter All Might.

All Might sees the potential in Deku and his inherent worth. The "Number One Pro-Hero" believes in and eventually loves the poor kid. Even while Deku was "quirkless," All Might showed him compassion. Kind of like how Paul pens that "… while we were still sinners, Christ died for us," (Romans 5:8b NIV). All Might didn't write Deku off; he rescued him. He trained him. And, within the first few episodes, he gives Deku One-for-All. All Might freely *gives* his "quirk" (superpower) to this unworthy crybaby. Because of All Might, Deku can finally change. He can finally be the person he was always meant to be: the best version of himself.

Let's tie it all in.

Jesus sees the potential in us even before we're born. Jesus tells us we are all worthy simply because we are His precious children. But He also knows we're human. We're flawed. Just like Deku, there is something missing from inside of us that prevents us from reaching our top potential. We can't save ourselves. By our own power, we can't even fix ourselves.

But Jesus loves us enough to fix that. He can save us. He can help us change! He lends us a bit of His own power through salvation and the gift of the Holy Spirit. And just as All Might didn't demand anything of Deku, neither does Jesus demand anything of us for His gift. He doesn't ask for payment; He just asks us to live our life for Him, just as All Might wanted Deku to live his life as a hero. They both called their respective acolytes to *be better*.

And I so desperately try. So does Deku. And you know what? We both fail. Deku doesn't always do what's right or best. He can't control his newfound abilities. He struggles. Such is the walk of a Christian—such is *my* walk. But just as All Might doesn't abandon Deku and keeps on trying to push the small boy to new heights, I know that Jesus is there to push *me* to new heights, too. Jesus has promised never to leave me. He's started a good work in me that He won't leave half-done. He *alone* has the power to save and change me: all I have to do is rely on him.

I'll close by throwing it back to Paul in Romans 7:24-25 (NIV), "What a wretched man I am! Who will rescue me from this body that is subject to death? Thanks be to God, who delivers me through Jesus Christ our Lord!"

Thanks be to God—because He saves us through Jesus's all-powerful might, and not through anything we can do on our own.

# RADICALLY LOVING, TRUSTING, AND HOPING: A HEART POSTURE

## BY SJ BARNARD

*"I can't leave you."*

— Conan

There are many Studio Ghibli fans, but Hayao Miyazaki is best known to my parent generation as the person who directed *Mirai shounen Conan*, or *Future Boy Conan*. I'm not from the Showa era, but I grew up watching the *World Masterpiece Theatre* (a series of animated classics adaptations), which was also where Miyazaki debuted, working as a storyboarder and animator. *Conan* was his first staple show.

Although it has nothing to do with the original book it's based on, I can safely say it's probably my favorite anime series of all time.

*Conan* is based in an apocalyptic world (a dystopia), and he grows up with his grandfather on a tiny island. Through a series of events, he comes to meet a diverse array of characters. What's so fascinating about Conan is that *no matter who they are, he reaches out to help them and trust them.*

On countless occasions, he is hunted down, jailed for something he didn't do, shot at, ect. But every time anyone is in need, he goes back to save them. It doesn't matter to him if the person was pointing a gun at him seconds ago. He'll still try to help them if they're in need.

Conan is a perfect example of Jesus's teaching in the Sermon on the Mount:

**You have heard that it was said, 'Love your neighbor and hate your enemy.' But I tell you: Love your enemies and pray for those who persecute you.**
**— Matthew 5:43-44 (NIV)**

And because he never changes this stance, Conan is able to positively affect those around him, even those who started out hunting his life.

But you might be thinking, "*I don't really have enemies. And it's not like this is 1st century AD that we get persecuted.*"

That's great! Although, I'm sure you'll come across someone who rubs you the wrong way. Or a random stranger who just swore at you for no reason. Or maybe, a family or friend you do love with all your heart, but they're sometimes... well, kind of annoying.

The thing to note here is that what matters is our heart posture. Where our heart is at will signify the action that comes out. Conan was able to help those in need because he genuinely cared for that person *all the time*. He didn't think of people betraying him because he wouldn't betray them. Even when they did, he trusted that person would want to choose the right thing in the end. And this hope and trust was what carried him through till the end.

This is the radical Gospel of Love Jesus has shown us.

READ 1 Corinthians 13, Romans 5:1-5.

1. Read 1 Corinthians 13 aloud. Was there a phrase or a verse that stuck out to you? Write it down.

2. What was the process Paul described in Romans 5 that leads to hope? How can we understand where hope comes from?

   How can you apply the principles of faith, hope, and love today? Is there a person you struggle to show love towards? What specific mindset and action can you show others today?

# SUGAWARA HUMILITY & CONTENTEDNESS

## BY MEGAN DILL

Do nothing from rivalry or conceit, but in humility
count others more significant than yourselves.
— Philippians 2:3 (ESV)

Not that I am speaking of being in need, for I have
learned in whatever situation I am to be content. I know
how to be brought low, and I know how to abound. In
any and every circumstance, I have learned the secret
of facing plenty and hunger, abundance and need.
— Philippians 4:11-12 (ESV)

It's so easy to get jealous, isn't it? A simple scroll through your Instagram feed might show your friends on vacation, getting married, buying a new car, etc. Even a conversation with an old friend can turn into a one-sided monologue about how successful they are. Have you ever been jealous of someone? Have you ever felt like they didn't deserve what they had?

Sugawara from *Haikyuu!!* has every reason to be jealous or upset. It's his last year in high school, and it's his last chance to play volleyball with his friends. But a new first-year joined the team and he's a better setter than Sugawara is. As a result, Sugawara has to watch from the sidelines as his last year in high school goes by. This is the part where he should be jealous or frustrated, right? Instead, Sugawara humbly accepts this change and whole-heartedly cheers for the team, including the new setter. He offers the team a lot of encouragement and waits on the sidelines to see if he'll get a chance to play. For him, this just provides motivation to get even better!

I don't know about you, but his reaction is incredibly convicting for me! He's not bitter, angry, or spiteful; in fact, he's supportive and encouraging. This is the kind of attitude we're meant to have when things don't go our way. We should lift others up, not bring them down. For Sugawara, the good of the team meant more to him than his own well-being. When something good happens to someone else, we should celebrate with them! Our faith in God should keep us content in any circumstance; we still have plenty to be grateful for!

Sugawara's response to his situation is humble; while he's frustrated that he's not on the court, he uses it to motivate himself to work harder! He doesn't complain and puts others before himself. We should aim to be as humble and as content as Sugawara is in whatever circumstances we end up in.

# NO GREATER LOVE

## BY AMY LYNN MCCONAHY

Greater love has no one than this:
to lay down one's life for one's friends.
— John 15:13 (NIV)

Sacrifice is a strong theme in the anime *Sailor Moon*. The Sailor Scouts battle many evils over the course of their journey, and within these battles there are many instances of one character sacrificing themselves for the good of the others. Whether it is Tuxedo Mask putting himself in harm's way to save Sailor Moon or Sailor Jupiter stepping in the way of an energy blast to save the others, this recurring theme of "glorifying sacrifice" can be found in every season of the anime. The Bible also glorifies sacrifice, especially sacrifice to save the life of another. In the words of Jesus found in John 10:11 (NIV), "I am the good shepherd. The good shepherd lays down his life for the sheep." In this passage Jesus was trying to explain to His disciples why He needed to die on the cross, to save them and the rest of us from evil. In *Sailor Moon,* the characters showed their love by sacrificing themselves for others. In the same way, Jesus showed us His love by sacrificing Himself for us. In 1 John 3:16 (NIV) it says, "This is how we know what love is: Jesus Christ laid down his life for us. And we ought to lay down our lives for our brothers and sisters." It is true that, unless you are in a high-risk job, you will probably never get the chance to die in someone's place. How then should we honor this "Greater Love"? We should honor Jesus' love and sacrifice by putting the needs of others first and putting ourselves last. This not only shows them our love, but the love of Christ as well.

# IN OUR WEAKNESS, HE IS STRONG

## BY ANGELA R. WATTS

Since teen hood, I always wanted to be like Captain Levi from *Attack on Titan*—unyielding, there for whoever needed me, and most importantly, strong. During my recent watch through of the show, however, I couldn't shake the shock!

Every struggle Jean Kirschtein had, I'd mirrored: fear of loss, grief over loss, fear in general, and the stubborn will to keep moving forward no matter the cost...even when we faced immense doubts. I always strived for Captain Levi's perfect exterior and unyielding strength...but so often, I'm weak.

> **For God hath not given us the spirit of fear;**
> **but of power, and of love, and of a sound mind.**
> **— 2 Timothy 1:7 (KJV)**

Is it okay to be scared and still fight? Is it okay to be in pain and still push onward? Is it okay to voice what I think and not be shamed by God?

I asked my brother as we watched the show, "Do you like Jean?" and my brother responded, "Nah. He thinks about morals too much." My brother is like Eren Jaeger—a hothead with a good heart who will do whatever it takes to win. On the flip side, Jean second guesses every move he makes, always seeking to make the best possible choice. It was ironic my brother didn't relate to the character I did. In Attack on Titan, Eren and Jean have a complimentary relationship and grow to be a power duo. My brother and I are similar!

But my brother's comment lingered. Is it possible for one to contemplate morals too much? Is questioning what is good or bad a weakness? Do I obsess over doing the right thing too often?

I don't think questioning our path is a sign of weakness. Overthinking and doubt are tricky things, and we shouldn't become obsessive over making mistakes, but there's no shame in being real with God. He's big enough to handle our doubts, fears, anger, and pain! He's also able to guide us through our journey every step of the way, and a heart seeking God's path is one that will be difficult to move down the road!

> Watch ye, stand fast in the faith,
> quit you like men, be strong.
> — 1 Corinthians 16:13 (KJV)

I try to be a strong person, and try not to let my doubts or fears control my life. That's partially why Jean's arc hits me so hard—he tries, hard, and he fails... but ultimately? He learns. He doesn't let things break him or leave him in the dust. He picks himself up and moves on. He's a prime example "of it's okay to be human and fall down, so long as you never give up." The questions we ask now might not be answered, but as our faith is tested, it can grow. We can stand even stronger in our faith in God!

**The wicked flee when no man pursueth: but the righteous are bold as a lion.**
**— Proverbs 28:1 (KJV)**

We can have moments of weakness and of anger and of regret. But we cannot live in these moments. Hold onto faith that God loves you, no matter what. 2 Corinthians 12:9 says, "And he said unto me, My grace is sufficient for thee: for my strength is made perfect in weakness."

Marco, one of the kindest characters on *Attack on Titan*, told Jean, "You're not a strong person, so you can really understand how weak people feel." Isn't that sort of the point of being courageous? It's not putting away our feelings or allowing them to control us. It's better understanding our world and choosing to do something about it, anyway. God doesn't tell us to have all of the answers, He asks only that we love and follow Him. That's enough and it will always be enough. Take heart and be of good courage... and fight on!

## BAKUGO'S PRIDE

### BY HANNAH CARTER

Pride goes before destruction,
a haughty spirit before a fall.
— Proverbs 16:18 (NIV)

If you watch *My Hero Academia*, it's hard to deny that
Katsuki Bakugo is filled with pride. He's been told his
whole life that because of his superpower, he's amazing.
He calls other students "extras," abuses Deku, and has
an attitude that no one else is quite as good as him.

But everything starts to change during the Kamino
Ward Incident.

Through a series of failures and personal blows, Bakugo is brought to his knees. He starts to realize that those around him might not be as worthless as he thinks—and that he might not be as *invincible* as he's always thought. It culminates in some heartbreaking character growth, and is a good reminder to all of us at just how deadly and dangerous pride can be.

I've heard pride called "the original sin" because pride is what caused the fall of Satan. He had the audacity to believe that he would be a better god than God Himself and got cast out of Heaven. And, in a way, I think pride is the "original sin" for another reason: because, from a young age, we are all filled with it. That's why following Jesus is sometimes so hard. We must *deny ourselves*, when even from birth, our most basic desire is to *indulge ourselves*. No matter how old we get, we are still fallen human beings with a desire to make ourselves god instead of God. And the end result of pride, no matter how it manifests itself, is death.

Bakugo's pride almost leads to his own physical death. Beyond that, pride can also spell death for other things: our happiness, our relationships, our walk with God, and so much more. I know I've probably put myself through a lot of needless hardship because I was too pridefully stubborn to back down from an argument. I've seen pride tear people away from God when they're disappointed with what He does or doesn't do, what He does or doesn't say, or even if He doesn't bless them in the way that they feel they should be blessed.

That's why it's so important to get this pride under control.

But how?

The first step is to acknowledge it and admit that, until we are in Heaven, we will probably always suffer from pride. It will wane with God's help, but we're still human. Pride is innate, and only God can help us keep it in check. So keep in mind that pride is a lifelong battle that we endure. Sometimes it frustrates me—there are days when I'm just too tired to fight—but then I remember that if I don't fight every day, I slip every day.

The second is to ask for help. Bakugo eventually has to do this because he can't save himself. Neither can we. It helps to have people who can give us reality checks and can mentor us in this journey. And don't forget the most important person to ask for help is God. Human assistance can keep us responsible, but only God can truly change our hearts.

The third is this: keep an open mind to how God might try and rid us of our pride. I know that no one likes to be broken or for bad things to happen, but sometimes, that's the best way we learn. Bakugo probably never would have defeated his pride (okay, let's be honest, it's still a huge struggle for him, but he's trying) if he hadn't been brought to his lowest point.

Accept these lowest points.

Embrace the fall when or if it happens.

Because when you reach your lowest point, you can only go higher from there. God can use these hard moments in life to build you up to heights you never thought imaginable, and the best thing is, you'll be a better person because of it.

Even though we may not all be as outwardly prideful as Bakugo, we all *are* prideful. But as long as we're still breathing, there's still time for a character arc of our own, and God is pretty amazing at writing those moments.

# HINATA GRATITUDE

## BY MEGAN DILL

Give thanks in all circumstances; for this is
the will of God in Christ Jesus for you.
— 1 Thessalonians 5:18 (ESV)

We've all had a bad day at some point or another in our lives. On those days, it's easy to get bitter and angry. We like to complain and blame others for our misfortunes. When was the last time you thanked God in the middle of having a bad day? It's easy to get blindsided by the bad things going on. However, there's always something to be grateful for, even on a bad day!

Hinata from *Haikyuu!!* has faced all kinds of obstacles while pursuing his dream of playing volleyball like the Little Giant. He wants to play even though he's very short. However, Hinata doesn't let that stop him! He might not be tall, but he can run fast and jump high. His middle school doesn't even have a boys' volleyball team, and he has to force friends to play with him just to enter the tournament. When he goes to high school, he learns that the volleyball team has lost its reputation as a powerhouse school. Everything seems to be getting in the way of his dream. But Hinata is simply grateful to be playing volleyball, to be on a team, and to have the chance to stand on the court! For him, the opportunity to fulfill his dream, even if he has to start from the very bottom, is enough!

Hinata's attitude during all of this is so optimistic and upbeat! Even when no one believed in him and the future seemed bleak, he was just grateful to be able to play. In some ways, Hinata resembles Job. Job went through all kinds of horrible things, but he also remained grateful to God for what he still had! The bad days might be rough. It might be hard to get out of bed sometimes. Even when everything in life seems to be going wrong, there will always be a reason to be grateful. It might be as simple as the fact that you're still alive, but that is definitely a reason to be grateful! In the midst of our struggling, we can still be grateful for the God who loves us and who sent His Son to die for us. If you have an optimistic attitude like Hinata, you'll always be able to find a reason to be grateful!

There have been a lot of times where Hinata had a lot he could complain about, but he remained grateful for the opportunity and decided he wouldn't waste it. Regardless of our circumstances, we always have a reason to be grateful. Don't waste your time in this life complaining about your circumstances; make the most of what you've been given!

# LOVE YOUR ENEMY

## BY RENEÉ LE VINE

Imagine this: a power-hungry psychopath has killed your closest friends *and* your lover, and if you don't stop her, she'll destroy your planet too. Your newest allies, whose own planet was destroyed by this psychopath, are certain she can't be defeated. She's just *that* powerful, *that* insane, *that* unstoppable. And she's got her sights on you, the only one with power to rival hers.

This is the situation Usagi Tsukino finds herself in in *Sailor Moon*'s fifth and final story arc, Sailor Stars. The powerful Sailor Galaxia, leader of Shadow Galactica, has conquered almost the entire universe—only our solar system, protected by Usagi and her fellow Sailor Senshi, is left. Usagi's new allies, the mysterious Sailor Starlights, are certain Galaxia is invincible. And once Usagi finally faces Galaxia, it's without her teammates or her true love Mamoru by her side. Face-to-face with the person who has literally ruined her life, one would think Usagi has every right to moon-dust Galaxia to infinity and beyond, without remorse. Right?

And yet, that's not what Usagi does. She cries over her lost friends, her lost love, her lost future. She fights Galaxia, giving it her all. But mercilessly killing her—the way Galaxia has done to those Usagi cares for—she does not. Even though we would expect Usagi to seek revenge, for Galaxia to get what she deserves, instead Usagi defeats Galaxia with the greatest weapon of all: love.

Rather than hit her with a sword or a magic beam, she reaches out a hand. Rather than rush forward in anger and revenge, she flies toward Galaxia with a smile, totally vulnerable, and without a word. In the end, her love is what saves the world.

God also encourages us to love those who ruin our lives. "'But to you who are willing to listen,'" says Jesus, "'I say, love your enemies! Do good to those who hate you. Bless those who curse you. Pray for those who hurt you.... Love your enemies! Do good to them. Lend to them without expecting to be repaid. Then your reward from heaven will be very great, and you will truly be acting as children of the Most High, for he is kind to those who are unthankful and wicked,'" (Luke 6:27-28, 35, NLT).

Loving one's enemies is no easy task. It even seems counterintuitive. But love has a power that can make even the impossible happen. After all, Usagi looks like the opposite of a hero—she's a selfish crybaby whose favorite hobbies are sleeping and eating. And yet, she has such a huge capacity for love that, without even trying, she draws people to her. It's why her fellow Senshi gladly lay down their lives multiple times to protect her; why Usagi and Mamoru's love for each other withstands monumental trials, giving each other strength in the process; why she encourages those she encounters to go on, whether it's the Starlights or her future daughter Chibiusa.

We too can show love's power—through God, who first showed us how. As the Apostle John writes: "This is real love—not that we loved God, but that he loved us and sent his Son as a sacrifice to take away our sins.

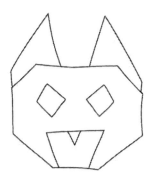

# SEARCHING FOR THE REAL FATHER

## BY RENEÉ LE VINE

One anime genre that is very popular in Japan is the *kaitou*, or "phantom thief," genre. While masked heroes in Japanese media go all the way back to the '50s with live-action shows like *Moonlight Mask*, the *kaitou* genre owes its popularity largely to the 1967 manga *Lupin III* and its many adaptations, which follow a descendant of French gentleman thief Arsène Lupin. Some phantom thieves, including Lupin, steal for the thrill, but others have a more noble purpose in mind. The Kisugi sisters of the '80s anime *Cat's Eye*—Hitomi, Rui, and Ai—are one of these. They lead a double life, running a café by day and by night stealing back their missing father's art collection, in hopes of finding clues as to his whereabouts.

The Bible doesn't condone theft, of course, however noble one's purpose for doing it. But like the Kisugi sisters, we too have a father we are seeking, even if unconsciously—our Heavenly Father. Thankfully, He rewards those who earnestly look for Him: "'In those days when you pray, I will listen. If you look for me wholeheartedly, you will find me. I will be found by you,' says the Lord. 'I will end your captivity and restore your fortunes. I will gather you out of the nations where I sent you and will bring you home again to your own land,'" (Jeremiah 29:12-14, NLT).

In fact, He not only seeks us, but *chose* us to be His. As He tells the people of Israel: "You have been set apart as holy to the Lord your God, and he has chosen you from all the nations of the earth to be his own special treasure," (Deut. 14:2, NLT). And rather than coming like a thief to take something from us, he brings us something better. As Jesus tells us, "[t]he thief's purpose is to steal and kill and destroy. My purpose is to give them a rich and satisfying life," (John 10:10, NLT).

The Kisugi sisters are noble thieves—the worst they ever do is knock people out with martial arts or sleeping gas, and some of the people they steal from are worse criminals than them (mostly mafia types). But when it comes to searching for our Father, let's use methods that *aren't* criminal, like the Bible and prayer. As Paul says, "What shall we say, then? Shall we go on sinning so that grace may increase? By no means! We are those who have died to sin; how can we live in it any longer?" (Romans 6:1-2, NIV).

# ENDEAVOR: A NEW FIRE

## BY DANIEL ANDRADE

At the beginning of episode 88 in *My Hero Academia*, we
see that Endeavor is met with a new and more powerful
Nomu; A Nomu is a deceased person who has been
infused with superpowers to be kept alive. This Nomu is
not just stronger than its predecessors, it is also obsessed
with power and is competent enough to make decisions.

In the beginning of the fight, Endeavor immediately
realizes that this fight won't be as easy as it was with the
other Nomus he's faced. Because of this, Endeavor
begins to fight away recklessly; he tries to finish the
battle as quickly as possible, but as the fight endures,

Endeavor pushes himself beyond his limits. Eventually, we find him on the ground pushed far beyond what he could handle; defeated. As the world was struck silent, a crowd in the distance ran, screaming in fear for their lives. They couldn't see Endeavor's flames burning, so they began to shout that there is no more hope; there is no more 'symbol.'

All of a sudden, a fire can be seen burning in the distance. Then a bystander yells amongst the crowd, "Don't just say whatever you want! Look over there! His flames are still burning! You know what that means? Endeavor is still alive and fighting for us! Don't say there's no 'symbol' just cause All Might is not here! Endeavor is risking his life for our sake; look at him!"

Many times, we lose hope when we don't see Christ in our lives. The disciples, after the crucifixion, went through a similar situation as we often do. After Jesus was crucified, Scripture portrays that it all felt like everything was over. No more miracles, no more hope. All they had in their mind was the death of Jesus. Even when Christ rose again, He walked amongst them and they didn't even recognize Him at first. As the testimonial accounts of the risen Christ were being proclaimed, Thomas, one of Christ's disciples, didn't believe the accounts because he hadn't seen Jesus, but eight days later, as all the disciples were gathered in that locked room, Jesus showed up. When Jesus was revealed alive, Thomas was permitted to touch the real wounds of Christ. As Thomas fell to worship, Jesus spoke, "Have you believed because you have seen me? Blessed are those who have not seen yet have believed," (John 20:29, ESV).

Do not count out God when we can't seem to see His flame burning. In 1 Samuel, Samuel was in the presence of the Ark of God, and while there, the word of God says that "the lamp of God had not yet gone out," (1 Samuel 3:3, ESV). Scripture makes it evident that the fire of God was dwindling, but before it could go out, God showed up (1 Samuel 3:10, ESV).

Jesus Christ is the light of the world (John 9:5, ESV) and the lamp to our feet (Psalm 119:105, ESV). It is only through Christ we are able to see what is before us. C.S Lewis says, "I believe in Christianity as I believe that the sun has risen: not only because I see it, but because by it I see everything else."

If it feels like your flame is dying, do not fret. Don't think that the hope you have is dwindling. Why? The fire of God has not yet gone out! Just as Endeavor's flame

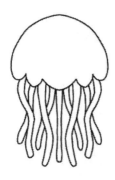

# BE WEIRD, BE TRUE

## BY E.N. CHAFFIN

In *Princess Jellyfish*, the Sisterhood is a group of otaku who shy away from anyone who isn't like them, especially the notorious stylish. They rely on themselves and keep to their hobbies, from trains to samurai to dolls. It is only when Tsukimi, who has a love of jellyfish, meets Kuranosuke that the Sisterhood's eyes are open to a whole world of amazement. She discovers that she doesn't have to hide away from the world just because she's different. In fact, she can influence the world around her using her love of jellyfish.

In the same way, children of God can influence the world. We can use our special talents and otaku hobbies to not only spread the word of God, but also help others understand it. We can also make sure our livelihood is protected from those who wish to hurt us because of who our Father is.

For instance, when the Sisterhood's home is in trouble of being torn down, their first response is to hide away in their house and not come out. A problem doesn't exist if you don't pay attention to it, right?

Wrong!

After badgering them nonstop, Kuranosuke convinces them to stand up and face their problem head on. He shows them that they can work with the world that is different from them without abandoning their otaku life. Christians need to do the same.

Whether we are spreading the Gospel or defending our right to worship the Lord, we need to work with the world we live in. However, we need to make sure we don't abandon our relationship with God and succumb to the world's ways. As it says in Luke, "What good is it for someone to gain the whole world, and yet lose or forfeit their very self? Whoever is ashamed of me and my words, the Son of Man will be ashamed of them when he comes in his glory and in the glory of the Father and of the holy angels." (Luke 9:25-26, NIV). We cannot stop worshipping God just because people in the world don't like it, exactly like Tsukimi shouldn't stop loving jellyfish just because some people in society find it odd. We also cannot deny our love for Christ, just as Tsukimi cannot deny her otaku lifestyle. Instead, we need to harness what we are given, nerdy hobbies and all, and show the world that we are weird and we are loved by God. If we can do that with our actions and our words, then we can influence the world around us in a positive and righteous way.

# ANN MAGNOLIA: LETTERS

## BY DANIEL ANDRADE

Miss Ann Magnolia is a 7-year-old girl whose curiosity is as great as any child's could be, she loves to play house, dance, solve riddles, play with her doll and even find bugs in the garden. One day, as she sat on a bench outside her mother's house, she saw Violet Evergarden. Miss Ann had never seen a real-life doll before.

Unlike any 7-year-old girl, Miss Ann is the daughter of a father who passed during the Great War and whose mother is terminally ill. During Violet Evergarden's stay, Miss Ann is held to entertain Violet while her mother rests due to her illness. As time passes by, Miss

Ann learns to trust Violet. She confidently comes to Violet with her curiosities and adventurous questions. Although everything seems to be fine, Miss Ann is very aware of what is soon to come.

s weeks pass, Ann questions her mother about the letters. She asks her whom the letters are for and why is it so important that they have to be written. Her mother could give her no words, and because of her silence, Miss Ann feels unloved. Immediately, she rushes out of her home, hurt that she doesn't know why her mother is dying. When she comes to a stop, Ann cries out that she isn't strong. She isn't a kind person. She even believes that her mother is sick because she is a "bad girl." Through her cries, Violet softly responds "There is no such thing as a letter that doesn't deserve to be delivered…"

Once the letters were finished, we see Miss Ann do all the things she wanted to do with her mother, but in a time lapse of one year, we see her mother disappear. Now, Miss Ann is alone, motherless and fatherless.

The Silence of God does not disprove His love towards us. The Bible says clearly that God loves us (John 3:16, ESV), but it is humane to believe He doesn't when life seems to go from bad to worse. Many

Christians struggle to believe in God when they see how cruel life can be, yet Scripture says "we know that for those who love God all things work together for good, for those who are called according to His purpose" (Romans 8:28, ESV).

We may never know what lies ahead in our life and we may never understand why God permits these necessary evils to occur, but we are comforted with the thought that God is ever present in times of trouble (Psalms 46:1, ESV). Even in times where we feel abandoned, God is a father to the fatherless (Psalms 68:5, ESV).

We won't always know why bad things happen, but in Romans 8:18 (ESV), it says "I consider that the sufferings of this present time are not worth comparing with the glory that is to be revealed to us." The Apostle Paul makes it a point to say that our sufferings will be the cause for God's glory in our lives. This means that one day we will learn why certain evils were necessary, and when we learn why, we will see God's glory shine even brighter.

When Miss Ann was left to live her life without her parents, she was definitely sad and hurt, but then she received a letter. As tears filled her eyes, Miss Ann read the letter she would receive from her mother on her birthday every year for the next 50 years. Every letter she received, though her mother was gone, made Miss Ann understand that her love for her went beyond her death.

The Bible is known to be called the "66 book love letter." When we feel lost, alone, abandoned, hurt or more, Christ shows us that his love goes beyond the cross and the grave.

As you open your bible, I pray your heart knows that all your letters will reach you no matter where you are.

## IZUKU MIDORIYA: CHOSEN

### BY DANIEL ANDRADE

In the beginning of the series, we hear Izuku Midoriya say "all men are not created equal." Even though he is making a reference to quirks (superpowers), I believe we, as Christians, do the same. We put ourselves down when we compare ourselves to others. We compare their gifts to ours, or we compare what they have to what we don't. Unfortunately for some, they are led astray because they don't feel 'good enough,' but in Christ, this is not the case.

In the first season of *My Hero Academia*, we are constantly reminded of Midoriya's quirklessness.

Everywhere he goes, he is shown to be weak. In the classroom, Midoriya is the only student without powers. He even carries a 'Hero Analysis for the Future' notebook despite being told that he will never have a quirk. Regardless, he still holds onto a dream that may never come true. Then one day, Izuku runs into All Might, his childhood hero, and asks him:

Izuku: "Could I ever hope to be someone like you?"
All Might: "...No, I honestly don't think you can become a hero without a quirk."

After Izuku's encounter with All Might, Izuku is distraught. He always knew the chance of him becoming a hero was slim to none, but after All Might denied him, he felt like there was no hope for him. As Izuku walks home sulking in the denial he just received, he sees a crowd of people. He looks to see a villain; it's ravaging and raging in a small alleyway as it tries to absorb Katsuki Bakugo's body and power. No hero present can help in this situation; they somehow don't have the quirk to stop it. Before Izuku could realize how dangerous the situation is, he runs quirkless towards the trouble because he couldn't just "stand there and watch [Bakugo] die."

After getting scolded by the heroes about his reckless actions, Izuku is met by All Might on his way home. As All Might reflects on the day's events, he tells Izuku that when he "saw this timid, quirkless boy try to save a life. It inspired [All Might] to act too." After this, Izuku is chosen to be the next heir to All Might's quirk, One-For-All.

As Christians, we all should aspire to be used by God. We all should desire to glorify Him with our gifts, but like I said earlier, some of us may lack gifts. In a world where people have extraordinary talents, sometimes we wonder if God can use us. In light of the first two episodes of *My Hero Academia*, All Might doesn't choose Midoriya because of a 'quirk'; neither does God choose us because of a gift.

**But the Lord said to Samuel, "Do not look on his appearance or the height of his stature, for I have rejected him. For the Lord sees not as man sees: Man looks on the outward appearance, but the Lord looks on the heart."**

**—1 Samuel 16:7 (ESV)**

Our gifts don't cause God to choose us; it's our hearts. When God had sought a king for Israel, he rejected what Samuel saw. He rejected man's standard to a king because man saw what looked good while God saw what is good. In 1 Samuel 13, it says that the Lord had sought out a man after His own heart (someone who seeks to please the Lord); that man was David.

This is the standard that God uses for us to be chosen. When Izuku Midoriya was chosen to inherit the quirk of All Might, Izuku had nothing to add to it. He had no quirk of his own, yet he was chosen because he had the heart of a hero. When God sent Samuel to Jesse's house, God chose David, not because of his gifts, but because he had a heart after God. Gifts aren't the reason God chooses to use us; it's our hearts.

# TRUST THE CAPTAIN

## BY HANNAH CARTER

"The captain is relying on us to follow his orders. If we believe in him, then we put our trust in his course of action. Do you have faith, Froppy?"
— Sirius, *My Hero Academia*

In Episode 32 of *My Hero Academia*, Tsuyu Asui (hero name: Froppy) finds herself at a dilemma in her internship. She's with another pro-hero, Sirius, while their captain, Selkie, is on a mission to save stowaways. However, it was actually a trap, and now Selkie is imprisoned by thugs.

Tsuyu's own instincts are telling her that she should go rescue Selkie, despite his explicit orders otherwise. She's stressed out and his instructions seem counter-intuitive to what she thought was the right or smart thing to do. But all the while, Sirius assures her that they're following the captain's orders, and they have to trust the man (seal?) in charge.

So when Sirius utters the words above, it struck me: in our lives, doesn't it always come down to whether or not we trust the Captain?

I'll be the first to admit that it is very hard to trust someone completely. Proverbs 3:5 (NIV) seems very hard for me to do: "Trust in the LORD with all your heart and lean not on your own understanding."

Don't trust my understanding? But...why? My own understanding is great. My own understanding makes me feel comfortable and in control. If I use the oft-quoted analogy of being in the car, I am the epitome of the "mom teaching the teen to drive." "Um, God? Are You sure You want to do this? Why don't You just let me take the wheel for a second..." (Insert various screaming noises as life gets very scary and unpredictable.)

It's hard for me to trust that what I hear is from God and not just a voice in my head. And it's hard for me to trust that He's got a plan. Not just any plan, either—it's hard for me to trust that He's got a good plan. A plan I'll like. It's hard for me to trust His timing when I feel like I've done nothing but wait. And, if I'm being honest, sometimes I'm a mix of impatience and anxiety.

*What if God never answers my prayers? It's within the realm of capabilities.*

*What if God answers my prayers, but not for years and years and years?*

*How do I know if I'll be happy or even enjoy His plan?*

*How do I know I won't be miserable or that He'll want me to do something I'm completely unprepared for?*

And it all usually boils back down to one question: *Will I be okay with trusting God no matter what kind of circumstances happen in my life?*

These thoughts are all just manifestations of my own trust issues. It's hard for me to walk blindfolded through anything, especially my own life—especially when I feel like I've been blindfolded my whole life with no clue where the end is at.

But that's exactly what the point is, isn't it? It's not trust if you've got all the answers or are relying on yourself. Life isn't about seeing the next twists and turns so you're prepared for whatever God throws at you. God even says in Isaiah 55:8 (NIV) that His thoughts are not our thoughts, and His ways are not our ways, so no one can predict or control Him. You just have to trust the Captain to guide you. It's about obeying His orders, even if they go against your nature.

Of course, at the end of the episode, Selkie's plans come through just as they should. The day is saved, and despite things looking hairy for a bit, everything turns out fine: *all because Tsuyu trusted the captain, even when things were at their bleakest.*

And... that's it.

That's what we have to do.

We just have to trust the Captain, and pray that His will be done.

# NAUSICAÄ AND PROPHECY

## BY JESSICA BERTRAND

Life is peaceful inside the Valley of the Wind, people go about their lives in harmony with one another. Outside of the Valley everyone knows about the encroaching trouble and all expect a savior to come and bring peace between mankind and the insects of the Toxic Jungle. Oh-Baba, a blind elderly woman, tells Nausicaä to expect one to come dressed in blue to save them. Lord Yupa spends his time, energy, and resources traveling to find their messiah. Who are you searching for?

Our Messiah came around 2,000 years ago in the form of a baby just like the prophet Isaiah said in Isaiah

9:6 (RSB), "For a child will be born to us, a son will be given to us; and the government will rest on His shoulders; and His name will be called Wonderful Counselor, Mighty God, Eternal Father, Prince of Peace." People expected a warrior prince to come and rescue them from their oppression under Ancient Rome. What God had in mind was something different. Instead, Christ chose to die for our sins and release us from spiritual tyranny. Isaiah 53:5 (RSB) said, "He was pierced through for our transgressions, He was crushed for out iniquities; the chastening for our well-being fell upon Him, and by His scourging we are healed."

Jesus loves us so much He was willing to die so could be reunited with Him. He wasn't what many expected, but Jesus is who we need. Lord Yupa and Oh-Baba were willing to step out in faith and hold firm in their belief of a messiah. We can believe too. Let's take it to Jesus.

*Come now, Jesus, and be our Guest. If it weren't for You, we wouldn't be here. Thank You for fulfilling the prophecy and promise of sending a Savior for my soul so long ago. Help me to walk with You in Your Word and Your way. In Jesus's name and for His glory, amen.*

# GIVING YOUR PAIN TO THE LORD

### BY JOSHUA REID

Pain, it can be anything. Emotional, physical, mental, or even spiritual pain; whatever form it takes, it's unpleasant. We try to avoid it as much as possible, but it comes either way. Unexpected but potent none-theless.

So, how do we deal with this pain? We, as humans, have several ways of dealing with our pain. We either suppress the pain, locking it away so it can no longer hurt us in the moment, or find other means to distract ourselves from the pain or we choose to barrel through it, believing we'll be just fine. However, what we don't realize are the effects of the pain. It can last longer than we anticipate and can follow us long into our teenage and adult lives if we don't rectify it.

Yet how do we deal with our pain when we don't know who to go to? In actuality, we do know who to turn to.

God can help us through our pain if choose to give it to Him. It's difficult to do because we as human beings don't want to appear weak in front of people, but there isn't much we can do by ourselves.

In the anime *Naruto Shippuden*, the titular character Naruto, in order to control the power of a demon fox trapped in his body since birth enlisted the help of another like him. But in order to completely take control of the fox's power, Naruto needed to first address the part of himself he thought he suppressed. His loneliness and pain embodied a darker mirror of himself in *Naruto Shippuden* episode #243 titled "Land Ahoy! Is this the Island of Paradise?" What's fascinating about how Naruto's pain and loneliness manifested as a darker mirror of himself is similar to how we as humans push down our pain instead of confronting it.

But what happens when that pain suddenly rears its head and faces us, what do we do? Do we fight it head-on only for it to repel us and keep us stuck in a cycle? Or will we choose to hand it over to God and let Him take it from us?

Unlike Naruto who had to come to terms with the pain and loneliness he buried in order to continue the process of controlling the fox, we don't have to. We can give that pain to the Lord if we choose to.

1 Peter 5:6-7 (NKJV) says, "Therefore humble yourselves under the mighty hand of God, that He may exalt you in due time, casting all your care upon Him, for He cares for you."

Giving our pain to the Lord isn't easy, whether because we believe that God can't heal our pain or because the pain has become a part of us, and we can't see any way out. None of that is true. When we give our pain to the Lord, we'll be surprised at how relieved we feel afterwards. It may not come instantaneously but it will happen.

## *COWBOY BEBOP* & UNEXPECTED UNITY

### BY NATHAN PETERSON

It almost sounds like a joke... A hyper intelligent canine walks into a spaceship. So does a feral teenager with mad hacking skills. And a flighty, shoot-first-ask-questions-never 77-year-old, who definitely doesn't dress or act her age. And a suit-wearing, gun-toting martial arts extraordinaire. Oh yeah, and don't forget about the grumpy, bell-pepper-cooking cyborg.

And somehow this ragtag mishmash of angst, apathy, and aggression is supposed to fly around the solar system hunting down bounties?

Trying to understand what holds *Cowboy Bebop's* main characters together is baffling. It's not like they work well together. They're often tripping over each other going after the same thing, or one of them just runs off on a random adventure while the others gripe and lounge around the ship. But at the end of the day, the crew of the *Bebop* always ends up back together. And in the final few episodes, it becomes pretty clear: they really do care about each other.

Up to this point, you may think I really didn't like *Cowboy Bebop*. Far from it. It's just... confusing. When you look at things logically, from an outside perspective, it just doesn't make sense how this group ended up together *and* stays together. But there's something endearingly, offhandedly, unexpectedly charming about them that keeps you as a viewer coming back for more, whether it's another glimpse into Spike's background, Edward's bizarre hacking abilities, or food gone bad taking on a mind of its own.

## A Call to Unity

This kind of inexplicable unity ultimately reminds me of the kind of unity the Church (I'm referring to the universal body of Christ here) is called to have. Once again, if you think about the Church logically, from an outside perspective, it doesn't quite make sense how all of us can somehow be bound together. We have different stories, different cultures, different passions, different longings, different priorities. We're separated across time and huge distances.

And yet of all the things Jesus could pray for us, He prays for unity, saying, "I have given them the glory that you gave me, that they may be one as [the Father and I] are one," (John 17:22, NIV). Paul builds on this saying, "There is neither Jew nor Gentile, neither slave nor free, nor is there male and female, for you are all one in Christ Jesus," (Galatians 3:28, NIV).

So what binds the Church together isn't an old fishing trawler turned spaceship or just the collective desire to catch a bounty to make some fast cash. **No, we are bound together by Jesus Christ himself!**

That's an even more baffling mystery that defies easy logic. And yet we know it's true. We know it's beautiful. It's something that ought to draw us back together—even in the midst of misunderstandings, in the midst of having conflicting desires and strong,

strong disagreements. Jesus is our rock, and He holds us together.

For non-Christians, when they see us fully pursuing this kind of unity, I hope it feels a lot like somebody watching *Cowboy Bebop* for the first time. It might even feel like a joke to them, that such a large diverse group could even pretend to get along. And yet the more they see the way we truly do love one another, they may find something endearingly, offhandedly, unexpectedly charming. Something that leads them to "praise our Father in heaven" (Matthew 5:16, NIV) and leads them to ask, "Who is this Jesus?"

For this reason, may we seek unity. It's not a joke. It's not a cutesy vision borrowed from a TV show. It's a prayer that comes from the very author and perfecter of our faith!

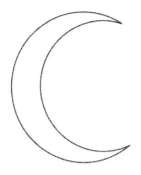

# NO ONE IS BEYOND SAVING

## BY AMY LYNN MCCONAHY

You, Lord, are forgiving and good,
abounding in love to all who call to you.
— Psalm 86:5 (NIV)

Serena Tsukino or Sailor Moon is a very unique heroine in anime in the respect that she sees redeemable qualities in her enemies. Whether it was Queen Beryl or Prince Diamond, she saw within them the ability to change, the ability to be someone good. Frequently, as Sailor Moon and the Sailor Scouts were about to unleash final judgment on the person of evil, Serena would plead with them to make another choice, to choose the good within them and leave the bad behind. Some of these enemies would choose the light offered to them while others decided to remain evil. These situations are very similar to God and His offer of forgiveness. God pleads with us to take the forgiveness that He offers because He loves us. Psalm 103:11-12 (NIV) says, "For as high as the heavens are above the earth, so great is His love for those who fear Him; as far as the east is from the west, so far has He removed our transgressions from us." God wants to take our transgressions, the evil we have done in this world, and make those actions as if they had never been. Just like Sailor Moon saw redeemable qualities in her enemies, God sees all of the redeemable qualities of His children. His forgiveness is free and absolute if we are willing to ask for it. Peter says this in Acts 10:43 (NIV), "All the prophets testify about Him that everyone who believes in Him receives forgiveness of sins through His name." Even as Christians we are in constant need of God's forgiveness for, we have all sinned, done evil, in some way. The task of sharing this forgiveness with others has been given to us by Jesus Himself as seen in Matthew 28:18-20 (NIV), "Then Jesus came to them and said, "All authority in heaven and on earth has been given to me. Therefore, go and make disciples of all nations, baptizing them in the name of the Father and of the Son and of the Holy Spirit, and teaching them to obey everything I have commanded you. And surely, I am with you always, to the very end of the age." In the eyes of Jesus is anyone beyond saving? The answer is a resounding no.

# THE GOSPEL IN NARUTO

## BY MORGAN L. BUSSE

For since our friendship with God was restored by the
death of his Son while we were still enemies, we will
certainly be saved through the life of his Son.

— Romans 5:10 (NLT)

Naruto. One of the longest and most beloved anime out
there. The story of an orphaned and unwanted kid with
the high goal to someday be Hokage (the leader) of his
village. He's stubborn, fights for what is right, a goof-
ball, and will never let go of his friends.

Even when they turn on him.

Over 500 episodes of *Naruto Shippuden* showed us that with his friendship with Sasuke.

Sasuke had almost everything: he was a powerful ninja in his own right, popular, and determined, even when he lost his clan. At first, he didn't want to have anything to do with Naruto when they were put on the same team. Naruto felt the same way, but then a friendship began to form between them.

However, Sasuke decided revenge was more important, revenge against the brother who murdered their entire clan. And revenge meant gaining power, no matter what it cost. As viewers, we watched Sasuke leave his friends and his village and seek out the villain for power. Hatred eclipsed everything in his heart. Every arc in the series Sasuke descended more and more into darkness.

In the meantime, Naruto also grew. He grew as a ninja, gained many friends, and led the way toward peace. But deep down, one of his main goals was to find his friend Sasuke and bring back from the dark path he had chosen. They meet up multiple times, each time Naruto chasing Sasuke, fighting with Sasuke, and calling him back. And each time Sasuke wounds him, whether with his words or physically.

But Naruto will not let go of his friend.

In the end, they team up to fight the ultimate villain. And they win. The world is saved, but instead of finding contentment in this hard-won victory, Sasuke turns on Naruto with the intent to murder him.

By now, I think the rest of us would go, fine, have it your way. I'm done with you hurting everyone and now you're even trying to kill me.

Instead, Naruto continues to pursue Sasuke. A big battle ensues between them. And to save his friend, Naruto uses his immense power and blows off each of their arms so that they can no longer fight. He gives up his arm to save his friend. And not just any arm but the one he uses to channel his special ninja power.

When my husband and I finished that episode, we sat back and stared at each other. There was the gospel, right there. No matter what, Naruto pursued his friend, intent on saving him. Even when Sasuke betrayed him and tried to kill him.

It reminded us of God. We were just like Sasuke, pursuing our own agenda, hurting those around us. We hated God, betrayed Him, and even killed Him. But He never gave up on us and gave His life for us. Just like Naruto did for Sasuke.

What a beautiful picture of love and sacrifice. I love finding these stories in our world, mirrors of the true story of God's love for us. And they encourage me to do the same.

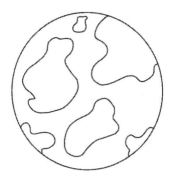

# STEWARDS OF THE EARTH

## BY RENEÉ LE VINE

The long-running *Pretty Cure* (*PreCure* for short) franchise has always been about light vs. darkness. The 2012 series *Smile Pretty Cure*, for instance, came out in the wake of the devastating Tohoku earthquake and tsunami of 2011, and encouraged smiling in the face of adversity. 2020's PreCure series, *Healin' Good PreCure*, likewise came at a fitting time, though unintentionally—at a time when climate change was on everyone's minds, not to mention the world having ground to a halt thanks to an unforeseen, crippling pandemic, what better than a series about healing the planet from virus-based baddies?

Like protagonist Nodoka and her teammates Chiyu, Hinata, and (later) Asumi, we humans were originally created to be stewards of the planet we call home. When God created man, he said, "... Be fruitful and multiply. Fill the earth and govern it. Reign over the fish in the sea, the birds in the sky, and all the animals that scurry along the ground," (Genesis 1:28, NLT). We are later told God placed Adam in the Garden of Eden to "tend and watch over it" (Gen. 2:15, NLT), a job he likely shared with Eve later. Once they sinned, however, the Earth shared in their curse (Genesis 3:17 NLT), and as Paul tells us, still suffers for it: "Against its will, all creation was subjected to God's curse. But with eager hope, the creation looks forward to the day when it will join God's children in glorious freedom from death and decay. For we know that all creation has been groaning as in the pains of childbirth right up to the present time," (Romans 8:20-22, NLT).

Nodoka, Chiyu, Hinata, and Asumi use the powers of nature itself to heal the Earth from the undermining attacks of the evil Byogens. We may not have such power, but we can each do our part to be better stewards of our planet. You don't have to go whole-hog and build a compost heap in your backyard and only drink out of metal straws (unless you want to, of course). It can be as simple as trying to recycle more, supporting conservation efforts, or planting flowers so that the bees don't go extinct. In fact, in *Healin' Good*'s last episode, when a side character points out that humans treat the planet just as badly as the Byogens, Nodoka and her friends are inspired to do what they can to do better—even without Cure powers. We can do so too. After all, the power's already inside us.

# NAUSICAÄ AND THE TOXIC JUNGLE

## BY JESSICA BERTRAND

Nausicaä's father was sick because he worked around the Toxic Jungle for so many years. The Toxic Jungle has spread over a vast portion of the world, it has found ways to permeate everything. The poisonous spores affect all who are near in and no one can hide from the pollution. Anyone who ventures near the Toxic Jungle must wear protective masks as exposure, even for a few seconds, runs the risk of lung damage.

Do you see how sin is like our Toxic Jungle? We can't avoid it. We naturally incline to do evil and ignoring sin or saying it doesn't exist denies the reality of needing a Savior. Sin destroys all it touches. 1 John 1:8-2:2 (RSB) says, "If we say that we have no sin, we are deceiving ourselves and the truth is not in us. If we confess our sins, He is faithful and righteous to forgive our sins and to cleanse us from all unrighteousness. If we say we have not sinned, we call Him a liar and His word is not in us. My little children, I am writing these things to you so that you may not sin. And if anyone sins, we have an Advocate with the Father, Christ Jesus the righteous; and He Himself is the propitiation for our sins; and not for ours only, but also those of the whole world."

Sin, like the Toxic Jungle, is invasive. If a few buds land on a tree and are not seen in time, the whole grove must be burned down. Our sins never end, like the Toxic Jungle. We have an escape from the contamination of sin and Jesus is our way to combat its encroachment into our lives. We're forgiven, loved beyond imagination. Jesus, our champion, is a loving, caring protector who conquered our sin. All we must do is ask. Let's take it to the Lord.

*Come now, Jesus, and be our Guest. If it weren't for you, we wouldn't be here. Thank You for saving me from the toxic sin in my life. Help me to recognize how to purge of sin from my life. In Jesus' name I pray, amen.*

# A MATTER OF THE HEART: HUMAN WILL VS THE HOLY SPIRIT

## BY H. S. J. WILLIAMS

Compassionate. Charming. A leader. A servant. For the people.

These descriptions do not suit a villain, and yet they are traits displayed by the antagonist of *Yona of the Dawn*, Soo-wan. Of course antagonists need only oppose the goals of the protagonist, without necessarily being a villain. Yet Soo-wan and the titular heroine, Yona, share the same aim—restoring the kingdom.

Throughout the anime and manga they often cross paths while doing the same thing to help others.

The difference lies in the heart.

Soo-wan made his stance clear: "I have no interest in the heavens, if all they can do is stand idly by. I look to the people. They will provide me the strength I need."

It's not that Soo-wan doesn't believe in divinity. He does. Painfully so. His heart is so bitter against the gods that he seeks to restore the kingdom himself without their help. He seeks to work out salvation by his own strength and the strength of mankind. And typically, as is human's tendency, his actions lead to extreme pain both for himself and the people he loves. A classic example of doing the wrong thing for the right reasons. Blood is on his hands. He has committed betrayal. And while some regret may shadow his heart, he is unrepentant. After all, as far as he is concerned, he must do what needs to be done. Setting his goals before love. In relying on his own strength and cunning while also giving in to the temptation of vengeance, he sacrifices everything.

Ironically, the actions he takes sets into motion the divine plan that he so despises.

Yona doesn't understand much about the gods yet, but she is willing to walk the path they set before her. She recognizes her own weakness. She realizes she is but a role in a much larger picture. Her heart is open, ready, and listening.

May we not be led by our understanding, pride, and ambition. May we always be teachable, our ear tuned to the voice of the Holy Spirit. May we always put His plan before our own.

For even the road to hell can be paved with good intentions.

And do not be conformed to this world,
but be transformed by the renewing of your mind, that
you may prove what is that good
and acceptable and perfect will of God.
— Romans 12:2 (NKJV)

Thus says the LORD:
"Let not the wise man glory in his wisdom,
Let not the mighty man glory in his might,
Nor let the rich man glory in his riches;
But let him who glories glory in this,
That he understands and knows Me,

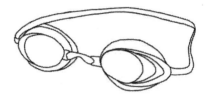

# CHOOSING TO BE FREE!

## BY ANGELA R. WATTS

I've struggled with rejection since I was a kid. Always the hermit and having no friends outside of my family, I dove into fiction to numb my pain. The first anime I completed was *Free! Swim Club* and *Free! Eternal Summer*. The anime was a fun escape, light-hearted with just enough angst that broke my aching heart, but challenged me to face my own demons.

*Free!* pushed me to set dreams and goals—even if I feared failing. Watching the characters face their fears inspired me. Some won and I rejoiced with them! Some failed and I crumbled with them. I still struggled, however. Why aim high if I might fall and crumble? Could I handle more rejection and broken dreams? Wasn't life hard enough without big hopes involved?

**Stand fast therefore in the liberty wherewith Christ hath made us free, and be not entangled again with the yoke of bondage.**
**— Galatians 5:1 (KJV)**

The characters of *Free!* didn't stop when things got difficult. They had to choose: freedom or bondage? Brokenness, or hope? Dreams, or merely existing? I saw Haru in his struggles with his friends and his future—and how Rin pushed him hard. It took a while for Haru to realize his dreams had changed, but that was okay. All that matters is we allow ourselves to dream and push ourselves to achieve our goals.

I strongly relate to Haru's trials: it was safer to go unnoticed rather than face rejection again. On top of my fear of rejection, I spent a large majority of my teenage years being a caregiver for my chronically ill mom. I numbed out and watched my life go on from the outside like a stranger looking in... But I'd always go back to *Free!* and the lessons it taught me. To go through life without goals or dreams means we suffocate the life in our bones. That's not okay!

Freedom doesn't come from drowning ourselves in fear or depression for the sake of feeling safe. Freedom comes when we challenge ourselves to be bold and have courage, even when we fall. Yes, we will fall. Rejection, pain, trials, they're all a part of life! *Free!* showed me that I was not alone, I was not the only one facing rejection or fear, and that even if I didn't seem as strong as others, I still had a place in this world! Just because I wasn't on the same journey as my fellow teens didn't make my journey less valuable.

> **If the Son therefore shall make you free,**
> **ye shall be free indeed.**
> **— John 8:36 (KJV)**

God is with us through the hard times, pushing us past our comfort zones and encouraging us to be courageous! If we follow His lead, we can be truly free. It isn't always easy, choosing freedom over fear, though if Haru, Makoto, Rin, and Sasuke taught me anything... Choosing freedom is always worth it. I do not have to choose living in fear that I'll be hurt or that I'll fail. I'm

God's beloved child, and so are you! Take your burdens to the Lord and choose freedom, choose hope, choose life instead of fear! We are free because of His greatest Gift. How precious is that?

> *"Gotta keep moving forward,*
> *far beyond the horizon."*
> — Rin Matsuoka

# TRUSTING TOSHINORI: OBEDIENCE OVER EFFORT

### BY A.D. SHEEHAN

Just about every shounen anime to ever grace our shores has heavily featured the training arc: the hero fights, fails, and must train harder to return and win. But like so many other anime tropes, *My Hero Academia* turns this idea on its head. Deku, our young protag-onist, finds his main opponent is the weakness of his own body. His inherited ability (*quirk*, in the show's lore), constantly threatens his body, and he must spend ten months training before he even receives this power, or he'll be torn apart.

We've all felt this struggle, battling our own weaknesses as we strive to do what God has called us to do, who He has called us to be. Like Deku, we can be extremely driven, but it's often not enough.

Thankfully, Deku isn't alone. His quirk donor, Toshinori Yagi, AKA All Might, is the greatest hero the world has ever seen, and he's there to personally coach Deku every step of the way. On day one he slaps Deku with the "Aim to Pass: American Dream Plan," a complete, daily routine incorporating exercise, diet, and rest.

In his own youth, All Might went through the very same thing, inheriting his power from his own mentor, so he knows exactly the challenges Deku is facing. If that sounds vaguely familiar, it's because Jesus knows exactly what we're going through, too. According to Hebrews 4:15a NIV, "For we do not have a high priest who is unable to empathize with our weaknesses, but we have one who has been tempted in every way, just as we are..."

You would think that Deku, the world's biggest All Might fanboy, would trust his hero's plan, but he doesn't. One day he collapses during a jog. All Might discovers that Deku has been pushing himself *too hard*, skipping sleep in order to train on his own, ironically undermining his training efforts with All Might.

This is a common theme in anime, perhaps a message to the overworked, overstressed kids of a Japanese culture obsessed with success. Slow down. Enjoy. Trust. You'll learn more and you'll get stronger if you rest appropriately. (See *Dragonball Z* for another example, noting the difference between how Goku trains Gohan and Vegeta trains Trunks as they prepare to fight Cell.)

But even if you're not an overworked Japanese kid, there's a message here. You have a Teacher who's been here before. He's asking you to do things far beyond your natural ability. But He knows you better than you know yourself. Trust His coaching.

We think we know how to get things done. We claim to know ourselves in that deep, secret place, so we push ourselves. Even in serving Christ, we try to outstrip Him, striving to work every moment, despite a clear command in scripture to rest regularly (Exodus 20:8-11). It leads to legalism, burnout, stress, and a false image of Christianity that has kept countless unsaved people from ever stepping into a church.

Instead, Jesus says this: "Come to me, all you who are weary and burdened, and I will give you rest. Take my yoke upon you and learn from me, for I am gentle and humble in heart, and you will find rest for your souls. For my yoke is easy and my burden is light." — Matthew 11:28-30 (NIV)

What could this mean? We still have the Great Commission, after all (Matthew 28:19-20). Like Deku, we have our own "beach to clean."

It means that more than our effort, God wants our obedience. Not only because it means we'll accomplish more for His Kingdom, but mostly because He loves us. Our mission is to serve Him, but His mission is *us*. When we obey, it means we trust. And trust is where we'll find ourselves most deeply in love with God. It's a close walk with Him, and we can't do better than that. We're not meant to.

Open that secret place to Him. Release your own ideas, even your own passions, and watch Him transform you into someone much greater than you could've been on your own. Go beyond Plus Ultra.

# DETERMINATION IS KEY

## BY E.N. CHAFFIN

*Haikyu!!* is the best sports anime. This comes from the fact that every character, including Hinata, has his or her own reason for playing volleyball and is determined to keep playing "for one more game" throughout the series. This determination is manifested best in Hinata himself. From the very first episode, the boy is looked down upon for his height and lack of knowledge about the game. He isn't talented or tall or on a proper team at all. Even when he gets to high school and joins the Karasuno team, Hinata still lacks the skills to be a good volleyball player. However, even with the odds stacked against him, even when players on his own team look down on him—both literally and metaphorically—Hinata doesn't stop playing. Sure, there are many characters that the audience sees who do quit. They either get tired of the grind or they believe they were never good enough. But Hinata doesn't. He is determined to play volleyball no matter what. In season two episode three, Yachi, the intern manager of Karasuno, suggests that Hinata must have his reasons to want to win. With fierce eyes and a no-nonsense attitude, he says he doesn't have a reason; he just loves playing the sport and wants to play more. Period. This is true determination. And throughout the series, it helps Hinata improve his skills and overcome failure. It makes him the best player in the show.

Just like Hinata, we Christians need to develop and wield determination like this for God. Even now in the world, we are being targeted for just believing. Sure, we can just hide the fact that we believe Jesus died for us and God loves us. But that would be so cruel to do to God. Instead, we need to have determination to hold fast to God and not to society, just like Hinata and volleyball, even if no one understands us. In Deuteronomy, we are told to "hold fast to" God (10:20,

NIV). We are also told in 1 Corinthians that a person "without the Spirit does not accept the things that come from the Spirit of God but considers them foolishness, and cannot understand them because they are discerned only through the Spirit," (2:14, NIV). Even if the world doesn't understand why we are so focused on God, it doesn't matter. We need to be Hinata-like. Period.

# THE UNEXPECTED POWER OF KINDNESS

## BY TEDDI DEPPNER

What is desired in a man is kindness,
and a poor man is better than a liar.
— Proverbs 19:22 (NKJV)

Tohru Honda is an orphan. Not only that, but she is homeless and living in a tent in the woods. She works part-time after school to meet her basic living expenses. If this wasn't enough hardship for one high school girl, she is targeted by bullies for simply talking to the wrong people. And then a freak mudslide buries her temporary home!

Someone experiencing such difficult circumstances might be excused for feeling sorry for themselves or complaining. It would be understandable if all their energies went toward the struggle to survive day to day. But the Fruits Basket anime (original manga by Natsuki Takaya) gives us a beautiful example of showing kindness to others even when we ourselves are hurting.

Day after day, Tohru is cheerful and optimistic. She works hard and doesn't look for handouts. When she accidentally discovers the secret lives of the family who take her in after the loss of her tent, she shows herself to be both trustworthy and kind. Instead of being horrified at the Sohma family curse, she accepts each individual for their unique strengths and positive traits. Overlooking their flaws, she supports them and befriends them.

Throughout the story we witness the tendency for hurting people to lash out at others. The members of the Sohma family have experienced a lot of trauma, not least because of how they have treated each other in response to the painful circumstance of their curse. Each individual Tohru encounters is either at the receiving end or the dispenser of harsh words, emotional manipulation, or even worse abuse. These deep wounds shape their personalities and motivate every choice and interaction they have. Will the sweet Tohru become trapped in the tangle of their twisted, dysfunctional lives? Or worse, will encountering their profound brokenness destroy her innocent optimism?

Many times in life my own hopeful optimism has collided with the despair and pain of the world around me. I feel small, powerless, and even ridiculous for believing things could be better. What good is a small act of kindness in the face of overwhelming tragedy?

The story that unfolds in the Fruits Basket series encourages me every time I see it. Kindness may appear small on the surface, but it is not powerless. Far from it. A single act of kindness can break down walls. Ongoing kindness in the form of loyal friendship can transform lives for eternity.

# REFERENCES

*Ann Magnolia: Letters* original version posted on Geeks Under Grace: https://geeksundergrace.com/anime-cosplay/ann-magnolia-letters/, submitted here with permission from Geeks Under Grace.

*Endeavor: A New Fire* originally posted on Geeks Under Grace: https://geeksundergrace.com/anime-cosplay/endeavor-a-new-fire/, submitted here with permission from Geeks Under Grace.

*Izuku Midoriya: Chosen* originally posted on Geeks Under Grace: https://geeksundergrace.com/anime-cosplay/izuku-midoriya-chosen/, submitted here with permission from Geeks Under Grace.

# ABOUT THE
# CONTRIBUTORS

**A.D. Sheehan** is the author of two fantasy novels, *Run the Mage* (in progress) and *A Legion of Gods* (currently seeking representation). When he's not losing sleep writing, he enjoys taking cars apart, trying to reassemble them, and racing with his local Rallycross club. Sheehan first discovered anime via Toonami in the late 20th century. *Dragonball Z*, *Outlaw Star*, and *Gundam Wing* were early favorites, followed soon after by *Cowboy Bebop*, *Trigun*, and anything by Miyazaki. He lives in Kansas City, Kansas with his two rusty

Japanese cars. Follow him on Facebook at A. D. Sheehan and Instagram at @SheehanFace.

**Amy Lynn McConahy** is a fifth-generation resident of a small town in Pennsylvania. She is a wife, mother of three rambunctious children, a church worship leader, and a majestic maven of the domestic domain. Above all, she is a child of God who is constantly seeking His light. While growing up, anime was a huge part of her life. It was not something that garnered widespread interest in her small hometown, but for her it was a window into a country that put OTHERS before SELF. This ideology strengthened her belief in Christ and made her into the "people-loving" person she is today. From Amy Lynn, "If my writing could give you something, I would want it to give you hope. Hope that things will get better. Hope that the sun will set on the evil and rise on the good. Hope that Love will conquer all." You can find Amy Lynn McConahy on Facebook and Instagram under "SunsetValleyCreations." For more info, check out: www.SunsetValleyCreations.com.

**Angela R. Watts** is the bestselling author of The Infidel Books. *The Divided Nation*, The Infidel Books #1, is endorsed by NYT and USA Today bestseller Lt Col Rip Rawlings and The Real Book Spy. She has published over nine books to date, with *The Mercenary's Deception*, The Infidel Books #3, releasing July 2021. When she's not writing, she's probably raising animals, painting, or working with her amazing editorial clients. She lives at Step By Step Sanctuary, Tennessee. You can find her on her website at angelarwatts.com or Facebook and Instagram @angelarwattsauthor!

**C.O. Bonham** is the pen name for a commonly misspelled first name. When she isn't writing stories of her own, she is busy reading stories by others. Her favorite stories are ones make you think and over think them. Stories worthy of wild fan theories. Visit her online at cobonham.com and on Facebook at @cobonham.

**Daniel Andrade** is a writer for Geeks Under Grace, a youth teacher and worship leader at his church, Family Life Ministries of Weslaco, and is also a geek who loves God, anime and video games! He started writing for Geeks Under Grace in February 2020, and in each article, he writes, he reflects on the situations presented in anime and how the Bible addresses them. He does this because he knows how it feels to struggle in trusting God, but through His grace, mercy and strength, I AM HERE (All Might Voice)! In any writing that's published in Daniel's name, he prays that it encourages others to continue pursuing Christ as others draw closer to Him. Read more of his articles at geeksundergrace.com and join the community, Geeks Under Grace Community, on Facebook!

**E.N. Chaffin** is an American author born and raised on country cooking and Japanese anime. She has made it her mission to upset the fiction world and change it for the weirder, moving even closer with each story she writes. Find out her plans to go plus ultra on her website www.enchaffin.com or on YouTube, Instagram, and Facebook @enchaffin.

**Hannah Carter** is just a girl who loves to dream and write. She currently has two published novellas, *Amir and the Moon* and *Seashells*, on Amazon. Her short story, "Lara," won a Reedsy competition. Her devotions and flash fiction stories have been published by various magazines and websites. Keep in touch with Hannah on

Instagram and Facebook at @introvertedmermaid3, or visit her at linktr.ee/theintrovertedmermaid3 to see her current work and subscribe to her newsletter.

From the beginning, **H. S. J. Williams** has loved stories and all the forms they take. Whether with word, art, or costume, she has always been fascinated with the magic of imagination. She lives in a real fantastical kingdom, the beautiful Pacific Northwest, with her very own array of animal friends and royally loving family. Williams taught Fantasy Illustration at MSOA. She may also be a part-time elf. Follow her @h.s.j._williams and www.hsjwilliams.com.

**Jessica Bertrand** resides in Colorado's Rocky Mountain Range. She's a budding author with an award-winning Colorado flash fiction piece. When she isn't writing, Jessica can be found volunteering for various church ministries, getting tangled in numerous knitting and crocheting projects, and doting on her family. You can find her online at www.jessicabertrand.com.

Christian. Writer. Historian. **Joshua Reid** is a longtime Christian and one who is still trying to figure it all out. A writer who doesn't mind asking questions until he finds the answer, Joshua enjoys writing stories that seek to honor the Father. He enjoys writing historical fiction, Contemporary, and alternate history. Having a deep love for the past, Joshua enjoys studying the past; especially when it pertains to the Bible. If you want to know more about Joshua, you can find him on his website at revivalthroughchrist.wordpress.com or on Instagram @joshuareidwrites.

Even as a young girl, **Kandi J Wyatt** had a knack for words. She loved to read them, even if it was on a shampoo bottle! By high school Kandi had learned to put words together on paper to create stories for those she loved. Nowadays, she writes for her kids, whether that's her own five or the hundreds of students she's been lucky to teach. When Kandi's not spinning words to create stories, she's using them to teach students about Spanish, life, and leadership. You can find her on her website at kandijwyatt.com or connect with her on Facebook and Instagram @kandijwyatt.

**Laura A. Grace** had a lifelong dream of getting to know authors behind the covers of her favorite reads. Little did she know that one day she would become one in the most unexpected way: a manga creator! She has since published *Dear Author: Letters from a Bookish Fangirl*, *Team Lines: A Poetry Collection*, and her debut manga, *Gathering Faith*, which will be releasing Fall 2021. A Tokyo enthusiast and avid MangaTuber, Laura creatively balances her passions of sharing her favorite indie reads on Instagram and regularly filming videos on YouTube to help and inspire manga creators to chase their dreams of publication. In between, she wields plastic lightsabers with her children and binge-watches anime with her husband. Come see what clean manga she is reading and recommending on her website, www.lauraagrace.com.

**Megan Dill** was born and raised in a rural part of Maryland, which is really just a nice way of saying that she grew up in the middle of nowhere. As a Christian, her faith is a huge part of her life and is incorporated into her writing. She spent her childhood lost in the pages of books, dreaming of fantastical worlds and crazy adventures. Her stories are clean and are typically fiction. As a lover of reading, she also loves to review and promote books by other authors! She has a Bachelor's degree in Business Administration: Marketing Analytics. When she's not reading or writing, you can find her watching anime, listening to k-pop, or spending time with her family and cat. Find her on Instagram @the_bookish_raven.

**Morgan L. Busse** is a writer by day and a mother by night. She is the author of the *Follower of the Word* series, *The Soul Chronicles*, and *The Ravenwood Saga*. She is a three-time Christy Award finalist and winner of both the INSPY and the Carol Award for best in Christian speculative fiction. During her spare time she enjoys playing games, taking long walks, and dreaming about her next novel. Visit her online at www.morganlbusse.com.

**Moriah Jane** strives to fill bookshelves with clean, high quality, and immersive stories. She writes fantasy, Gaslamp being her favorite, and loves writing for young adult and middle grade readers. She also enjoys drawing characters and wearing Victorian-eques clothing. Connect with her on Facebook or on Instagram @moriah_jane.

**Nathan Peterson** is an aspiring novelist and artist. Growing up with a passion for all things Star Wars and Lord of the Rings, it's no surprise he loves weaving sci-fi, fantasy, and real life into his stories. Check out his comic book series that he co-wrote and co-illustrated: Vidar & Hans (vidarandhans.wordpress.com) following the antics and adventures of a Viking and troll aspiring to be superheroes in a small town in Wisconsin.

**Reneé Le Vine** is a writer of fantasy and science fiction. She has always loved story, and spent much of her cable-free childhood reading everything she could find. Later on, she turned this passion for words into writing of her own, from stories about baby-sitting imaginary children to multiple NaNoWriMo-winning novels. When not reading or writing, she can be found listening to music, playing video games, or watching anime (the more obscure, the better). Levine writes from the San Diego area. Visit her online at www.reneedlevine.com.

**SJ Barnard** is a Classics loving YA author with a penchant for drinking a cup of too many Earl Greys. She dreams of type-writers, sumikko-gurashi (corner living), and minimalism. Her favourite manga artist of all time is Tezuka Osamu, and have lived in his "home" city, Takadano-baba. You can find her on her blog, sjbarnard.blog or drooling over books on her Instagram @logosbarnard.

**Teddi Deppner** is a published indie author and co-founder of Havok Publishing. She's also a homeschool mom of two teens and an avid toy photographer. Hear more about her projects at www.TeddiDeppner.com or connect on Twitter and Instagram @teddideppner.

# BE THE FIRST TO HEAR ABOUT FUTURE *FINDING GOD IN ANIME* ANTHOLOGIES!

Sign up for announcements for
when submissions will open!

LauraAGrace.com/FindingGodInAnime

Made in the USA
Columbia, SC
27 May 2021